THIS BUCKET LIST JOURNAL
BELONGS TO:

_____

OUR SEXUAL BUCKET LIST

THANK YOU SO MUCH FOR YOUR PURCHASE, THE AIM OF THIS BOOK IS TO BRING YOU CLOSER TOGETHER, NOT JUST PHYSICALLY BUT MENTALLY AND SPIRITUALLY AS WELL.

YOU CAN USE THIS BOOK TO;

- RETURN THE SPARK TO THE BEDROOM
- EXPLORE EACH OTHERS BOUNDARIES
- GIVE YOU IDEAS TO TRY
- CREATE MEMORIES TO LOOK BACK ON, ETC

PLEASE COMPLETE THE CHALLENGES IN THIS BOOK ONLY IF YOU **FEEL COMFORTABLE** WITH THEM IF NOT THEN FEEL FREE TO SKIP THEM, UNDERSTAND THAT PEOPLE ARE AT DIFFERENT SEXUAL STAGES IN THEIR LIVES, AND ALSO THAT SOME PEOPLE ARE MORE RESERVED THAN OTHERS AND THAT'S TOTALLY FINE.

YOU CAN ALSO COMPLETE THE CHALLENGES IN ANY ORDER YOU WISH, SIMPLY TICK THEM OFF AS YOU GO.

FOR EVERY CHALLENGE THERE IS ALSO A SEXUAL SURVEY FOR YOU BOTH TO FILL OUT TOGETHER,

THIS INCLUDES;

- HIS AND HER THOUGHTS ON THE CHALLENGE BEFORE
- HIS AND HER THOUGHTS ON THE CHALLENGE AFTER
- HIS AND HER SEPARATE RATING OF THE CHALLENGE
- WHETHER YOU WOULD LIKE TO TRY THIS TASK AGAIN

FOR EACH CHALLENGE THERE IS ALSO A JOURNAL PAGE FOR YOU BOTH TO FILL OUT TOGETHER, **RELIVE THE SEXY MOMENT** AND WRITE DOWN IN DETAIL EVERYTHING THAT HAPPENED, FAVOURITE PARTS, WHERE IT TOOK PLACE. THINKING AND READING ABOUT A PAST CHALLENGE CAN BE A HUGE TURN ON SO LOOK BACK AND USE IT TO GET YOUR HEARTS RACING.

FINALLY IF YOU ARE ADVANCED ENOUGH AND CAN STORE THE BOOK IN A SAFE PLACE, TAKE SOME PICTURES DURING THE CHALLENGE, PRINT THEM OUT AND STICK THEM ON THE PICTURES AND MEMORIES PAGE. AFTER YOU HAVE COMPLETED ALL OF THE CHALLENGES YOU LIKE, YOU CAN USE IT AS A **SEXUAL SCRAPBOOK** TO LOOK BACK ON.

OUR SEXUAL BUCKET LIST

	CHOOSE AND BUY A SEX TOY FOR EACH OTHER, WHEN IT ARRIVES USE IT ON EACH OTHER.
	THE WOMAN BLINDFOLDS THE MAN AND HE MUST LICK, NIBBLE OR SUCK ANYTHING THAT IS PUT IN FRONT OF HIM.
	FOOD SEX - INVOLVE ANYTHING EDIBLE, SUCH AS CHOCOLATE SAUCE, WHIPPED CREAM, BANANAS, STRAWBERRIES, HONEY.
	TEASE YOUR LOVER BY RANDOMLY SENDING 5 RAUNCHY PICS WHILST THEY ARE AT WORK, INCREASE THE NAUGHTYNESS WITH EACH PIC.
	WATCH SOME PORN TOGETHER – CHOOSE A NIGHT AND DISCUSS WHAT YOU WOULD LIKE TO SEE OR WOULDN'T.
	THE WOMAN MUST TAKE CHARGE AND USE HIS HANDS AS HER OWN AND STIMULATE HERSELF TO REACH AN ORGASM.
	HAVE SEX OUTSIDE – THINK BACK SEAT OF YOUR CAR, IN THE SEA, YOUR GARDEN, A CHANGING ROOM.
	TALK DIRTY TO EACH OTHER WHILE GETTING INTIMATE, TELL EACH OTHER WHAT YOU WANT TO DO TO EACH OTHER OR WHAT YOU WANT TO THEM TO DO TO YOU.
	LISTEN TO AN EROTIC STORY TOGETHER VIA AUDIBLE ETC – THIS CAN BE DAILY / WEEKLY OR AS A ONE OFF.
	TOUCH, LICK, KISS EACH OTHER ANYWHERE – EXCLUDING BREASTS AND PRIVATES – TRY TO HOLD OUT FOR 20 MINUTES AND THEN ANYTHING GOES.
	BONDAGE – THE WOMAN GETS TO TIE THE MAN UP AND DO AS SHE WISHES.
	WITH YOUR CLOTHES ON PASSIONATELY KISS EACH OTHER FOR AS LONG AS POSSIBLE, YOUR BODIES CAN TOUCH BUT YOU CAN'T USE YOUR HANDS – HOLD OUT FOR 20 MINUTES THEN ANYTHING GOES.
	HAVE SEX IN THE SHOWER – START BY WASHING EACH OTHER'S BODIES.
	ROLE PLAY – DISCUSS A SCENARIO AND ACT IT OUT (STRANGERS AT A BAR, PLUMBER COMING OVER TO FIX SOMETHING, NURSE, A NAUGHTY MASSAGE) WHAT EVER YOU CHOOSE, PRETEND YOU'VE NEVER MET.
	HAVE A SAFE THREESOME – PURCHASE A DILDO WITH A SUCTION PAD, STICK IT TO THE BATHROOM TILES, SHE CAN SUCK IT WHILE HE FUCKS HER OR SHE CAN SUCK HIM WHILE FUCKING THE DILDO.

OUR SEXUAL BUCKET LIST

	BOTH PLAY WITH YOURSELF AND REACH ORGASM WHILST NEXT TO EACH OTHER – YOU CAN LOOK BUT YOU CAN'T TOUCH EACH OTHER.
	THE WOMAN MUST GREET HIM WHEN HE COMES HOME FROM WORK BY WEARING SOMETHING VERY SEXY OR NOTHING AT ALL.
	THE MAN MUST GIVE HER A FULL BODY MASSAGE USING OIL – YOU MUST BOTH BE NAKED – LET THE SEXUAL TENSION RISE BY NOT TOUCHING ANYWHERE INTIMATE FOR AT LEAST 15 MINUTES.
	THE MAN MUST RANDOMLY PERFORM ORAL SEX ON HER – THIS COULD BE WHILST ON THE SOFA WATCHING TV, FIRST THING IN THE MORNING, WHILE SHE IS APPLYING HER MAKE UP ETC
	WHEN YOU ARE IN A CAR OR TAXI TOGETHER LET YOUR HANDS WANDER WITHOUT ANYONE SEEING.
	THE MAN IS GIVEN PERMISSION TO TAKE PICTURES OF HER – SHE MUST FOLLOW HIS DIRECTION FOR POSITIONS AND TAKE ITEMS OFF AS HE REQUESTS, SHE MUST ALSO DO ANYTHING SEXUAL THAT HE ASKS.
	FILM YOURSELVES WHILE PERFORMING ORAL ON EACH OTHER AND HAVING SEX.
	HAVE SEX SOMEWHERE IN YOUR HOUSE BUT NOT A BEDROOM – THINK OFFICE, STAIRS, KITCHEN TABLE, UTILITY ROOM
	HIDE YOUR FACES AND VISIT AN ADULT SITE SUCH AS OMEGLE OR CHAT ROULETTE AND PERFORM FOR SOMEONE ON WEBCAM – YOU CAN GO AS FAR AS YOU FEEL COMFORTABLE WITH.
	BE ROUGH WITH EACH OTHER – PUSH HIM ON THE BED, PULL HER HAIR, LIGHT CHOKING, SPANKING – DISCUSS A SAFE WORD BEFORE THAT WILL END THE SESSION.
	THE WOMAN MUST RANDOMLY PERFORM ORAL SEX ON HIM – THIS COULD BE WHILST HE'S SLEEPING, ON HIS PHONE, WHEN HE GETS OUT OF THE SHOWER.
	THE WOMAN GETS TO TIE HIM UP AND DO AS SHE WISHES
	USE ICE CUBES ON EACH OTHER'S BODIES
	THE MAN MUST RUN HER A ROMANTIC BATH (WITH CANDLES, BATH BOMBS ETC) THEN GIVE HER A NECK, BACK MASSAGE THEN FINALLY PERFORM ORAL SEX ON HER
	BONDAGE – THE MAN GETS TO TIE HER UP AND DO AS HE WISHES TO HER

OUR SEXUAL BUCKET LIST

WRITE DOWN AT LEAST 3 THINGS EACH BELOW THAT YOU WOULD LIKE TO TRY, EG; ANAL PLAY, FANTASIES, OUTFITS, PLACES TO HAVE SEX ETC. COMPLETE THEM LIKE YOU DID THE OTHER TASKS.

HER :

HER :

HER :

HER :

HER :

HIM :

HIM :

HIM :

HIM :

HIM :

OUR SEXUAL BUCKET LIST

WHICH
TASK :

HER THOUGHTS BEFORE :

_____

_____

_____

_____

HIS THOUGHTS BEFORE :

_____

_____

_____

_____

COMPLETED

DATE :

HER THOUGHTS AFTER :

HIS THOUGHTS AFTER :

HER RATING (1 – 10)

HIS RATING (1 – 10)

I WOULD LIKE TO DO IT AGAIN

I WOULD LIKE TO DO IT AGAIN

OUR JOURNAL

DESCRIBE IN DETAIL EVERY PART OF THE EVENT
WHAT HAPPENED? HOW? WHERE? WHAT DID YOU LIKE?

PICTURES & MEMORIES

PRINT OUT A FEW PICTURES AND STICK
THEM HERE TO BRING BACK MEMORIES OF
THE SEXY EVENT

OUR SEXUAL BUCKET LIST

WHICH
TASK :

HER THOUGHTS BEFORE :   HIS THOUGHTS BEFORE :

_____   _____

_____   _____

_____   _____

_____   _____

COMPLETED

DATE :

HER THOUGHTS AFTER :   HIS THOUGHTS AFTER :

HER RATING (1 – 10)   HIS RATING (1 – 10)

I WOULD LIKE TO DO IT AGAIN   I WOULD LIKE TO DO IT AGAIN

OUR JOURNAL

DESCRIBE IN DETAIL EVERY PART OF THE EVENT
WHAT HAPPENED? HOW? WHERE? WHAT DID YOU LIKE?

_____

_____

_____

_____

_____

_____

_____

_____

_____

_____

_____

_____

_____

_____

_____

_____

_____

_____

_____

PICTURES & MEMORIES

PRINT OUT A FEW PICTURES AND STICK
THEM HERE TO BRING BACK MEMORIES OF
THE SEXY EVENT

OUR SEXUAL BUCKET LIST

WHICH
TASK :

HER THOUGHTS BEFORE :

_____

_____

_____

_____

HIS THOUGHTS BEFORE :

_____

_____

_____

_____

COMPLETED

DATE :

HER THOUGHTS AFTER :

HIS THOUGHTS AFTER :

HER RATING (1 – 10)

HIS RATING (1 – 10)

I WOULD LIKE TO DO IT AGAIN

I WOULD LIKE TO DO IT AGAIN

OUR JOURNAL

PICTURES & MEMORIES

PRINT OUT A FEW PICTURES AND STICK
THEM HERE TO BRING BACK MEMORIES OF
THE SEXY EVENT

OUR SEXUAL BUCKET LIST

WHICH
TASK :

HER THOUGHTS BEFORE :   HIS THOUGHTS BEFORE :

_____   _____

_____   _____

_____   _____

_____   _____

COMPLETED

DATE :

HER THOUGHTS AFTER :   HIS THOUGHTS AFTER :

HER RATING (1 – 10)   HIS RATING (1 – 10)

I WOULD LIKE TO DO IT AGAIN   I WOULD LIKE TO DO IT AGAIN

OUR JOURNAL

DESCRIBE IN DETAIL EVERY PART OF THE EVENT
WHAT HAPPENED? HOW? WHERE? WHAT DID YOU LIKE?

_____

_____

_____

_____

_____

_____

_____

_____

_____

_____

_____

_____

_____

_____

_____

_____

_____

_____

PICTURES & MEMORIES

PRINT OUT A FEW PICTURES AND STICK
THEM HERE TO BRING BACK MEMORIES OF
THE SEXY EVENT

OUR SEXUAL BUCKET LIST

WHICH
TASK :

HER THOUGHTS BEFORE :

_____

_____

_____

_____

HIS THOUGHTS BEFORE :

_____

_____

_____

_____

COMPLETED

DATE :

HER THOUGHTS AFTER :

HIS THOUGHTS AFTER :

HER RATING (1 – 10)

☐

HIS RATING (1 – 10)

☐

I WOULD LIKE TO DO IT AGAIN

☐

I WOULD LIKE TO DO IT AGAIN

☐

OUR JOURNAL

DESCRIBE IN DETAIL EVERY PART OF THE EVENT
WHAT HAPPENED? HOW? WHERE? WHAT DID YOU LIKE?

_____

_____

_____

_____

_____

_____

_____

_____

_____

_____

_____

_____

_____

_____

_____

_____

_____

_____

_____

_____

_____

PICTURES & MEMORIES

PRINT OUT A FEW PICTURES AND STICK
THEM HERE TO BRING BACK MEMORIES OF
THE SEXY EVENT

OUR SEXUAL BUCKET LIST

WHICH
TASK :

HER THOUGHTS BEFORE :

HIS THOUGHTS BEFORE :

_____

_____

_____

_____

_____

_____

_____

_____

COMPLETED

DATE :

HER THOUGHTS AFTER :

HIS THOUGHTS AFTER :

HER RATING (1 – 10)

HIS RATING (1 – 10)

☐

☐

I WOULD LIKE TO DO IT AGAIN

I WOULD LIKE TO DO IT AGAIN

☐

☐

OUR JOURNAL

_____

_____

_____

_____

_____

_____

_____

_____

_____

_____

_____

_____

_____

_____

_____

_____

_____

PICTURES & MEMORIES

PRINT OUT A FEW PICTURES AND STICK
THEM HERE TO BRING BACK MEMORIES OF
THE SEXY EVENT

OUR SEXUAL BUCKET LIST

WHICH
TASK :

HER THOUGHTS BEFORE :

_____

_____

_____

_____

HIS THOUGHTS BEFORE :

_____

_____

_____

_____

COMPLETED

DATE :

HER THOUGHTS AFTER :

HIS THOUGHTS AFTER :

HER RATING (1 – 10)

☐

HIS RATING (1 – 10)

☐

I WOULD LIKE TO DO IT AGAIN

☐

I WOULD LIKE TO DO IT AGAIN

☐

OUR JOURNAL

DESCRIBE IN DETAIL EVERY PART OF THE EVENT
WHAT HAPPENED? HOW? WHERE? WHAT DID YOU LIKE?

PICTURES & MEMORIES

PRINT OUT A FEW PICTURES AND STICK
THEM HERE TO BRING BACK MEMORIES OF
THE SEXY EVENT

OUR SEXUAL BUCKET LIST

WHICH
TASK :

HER THOUGHTS BEFORE :

_____

_____

_____

_____

HIS THOUGHTS BEFORE :

_____

_____

_____

_____

COMPLETED

DATE :

HER THOUGHTS AFTER :

HIS THOUGHTS AFTER :

HER RATING (1 – 10)

HIS RATING (1 – 10)

I WOULD LIKE TO DO IT AGAIN

I WOULD LIKE TO DO IT AGAIN

OUR JOURNAL

DESCRIBE IN DETAIL EVERY PART OF THE EVENT
WHAT HAPPENED? HOW? WHERE? WHAT DID YOU LIKE?

_____

_____

_____

_____

_____

_____

_____

_____

_____

_____

_____

_____

_____

_____

_____

_____

_____

PICTURES & MEMORIES

PRINT OUT A FEW PICTURES AND STICK
THEM HERE TO BRING BACK MEMORIES OF
THE SEXY EVENT

OUR SEXUAL BUCKET LIST

WHICH
TASK :

HER THOUGHTS BEFORE :

_____

_____

_____

_____

HIS THOUGHTS BEFORE :

_____

_____

_____

_____

COMPLETED

DATE :

HER THOUGHTS AFTER :

HIS THOUGHTS AFTER :

HER RATING (1 – 10)

☐

HIS RATING (1 – 10)

☐

I WOULD LIKE TO DO IT AGAIN

☐

I WOULD LIKE TO DO IT AGAIN

☐

OUR JOURNAL

DESCRIBE IN DETAIL EVERY PART OF THE EVENT
WHAT HAPPENED? HOW? WHERE? WHAT DID YOU LIKE?

PICTURES & MEMORIES

PRINT OUT A FEW PICTURES AND STICK
THEM HERE TO BRING BACK MEMORIES OF
THE SEXY EVENT

OUR SEXUAL BUCKET LIST

WHICH
TASK :

HER THOUGHTS BEFORE :   HIS THOUGHTS BEFORE :

_____   _____

_____   _____

_____   _____

_____   _____

COMPLETED

DATE :

HER THOUGHTS AFTER :   HIS THOUGHTS AFTER :

HER RATING (1 – 10)   HIS RATING (1 – 10)

┌─────────┐   ┌─────────┐
│   │   │   │
└─────────┘   └─────────┘

I WOULD LIKE TO DO IT AGAIN   I WOULD LIKE TO DO IT AGAIN

┌─────────┐   ┌─────────┐
│   │   │   │
└─────────┘   └─────────┘

OUR JOURNAL

DESCRIBE IN DETAIL EVERY PART OF THE EVENT
WHAT HAPPENED? HOW? WHERE? WHAT DID YOU LIKE?

_____

_____

_____

_____

_____

_____

_____

_____

_____

_____

_____

_____

_____

_____

_____

_____

PICTURES & MEMORIES

PRINT OUT A FEW PICTURES AND STICK
THEM HERE TO BRING BACK MEMORIES OF
THE SEXY EVENT

OUR SEXUAL BUCKET LIST

WHICH
TASK :

HER THOUGHTS BEFORE :

HIS THOUGHTS BEFORE :

_____

_____

_____

_____

_____

_____

_____

COMPLETED

DATE :

HER THOUGHTS AFTER :

HIS THOUGHTS AFTER :

HER RATING (1 – 10)

HIS RATING (1 – 10)

I WOULD LIKE TO DO IT AGAIN

I WOULD LIKE TO DO IT AGAIN

OUR JOURNAL

DESCRIBE IN DETAIL EVERY PART OF THE EVENT
WHAT HAPPENED? HOW? WHERE? WHAT DID YOU LIKE?

PICTURES & MEMORIES

PRINT OUT A FEW PICTURES AND STICK
THEM HERE TO BRING BACK MEMORIES OF
THE SEXY EVENT

OUR SEXUAL BUCKET LIST

WHICH
TASK :

HER THOUGHTS BEFORE :

HIS THOUGHTS BEFORE :

_____

_____

_____

_____

_____

_____

_____

_____

COMPLETED

DATE :

HER THOUGHTS AFTER :

HIS THOUGHTS AFTER :

HER RATING (1 – 10)

HIS RATING (1 – 10)

I WOULD LIKE TO DO IT AGAIN

I WOULD LIKE TO DO IT AGAIN

OUR JOURNAL

DESCRIBE IN DETAIL EVERY PART OF THE EVENT
WHAT HAPPENED? HOW? WHERE? WHAT DID YOU LIKE?

_____

_____

_____

_____

_____

_____

_____

_____

_____

_____

_____

_____

_____

_____

_____

_____

_____

_____

PICTURES & MEMORIES

PRINT OUT A FEW PICTURES AND STICK
THEM HERE TO BRING BACK MEMORIES OF
THE SEXY EVENT

OUR SEXUAL BUCKET LIST

WHICH
TASK :

HER THOUGHTS BEFORE :

_____

_____

_____

_____

HIS THOUGHTS BEFORE :

_____

_____

_____

_____

COMPLETED

DATE :

HER THOUGHTS AFTER :

HIS THOUGHTS AFTER :

HER RATING (1 – 10)

HIS RATING (1 – 10)

I WOULD LIKE TO DO IT AGAIN

I WOULD LIKE TO DO IT AGAIN

OUR JOURNAL

DESCRIBE IN DETAIL EVERY PART OF THE EVENT
WHAT HAPPENED? HOW? WHERE? WHAT DID YOU LIKE?

_____

_____

_____

_____

_____

_____

_____

_____

_____

_____

_____

_____

_____

_____

_____

_____

_____

_____

_____

PICTURES & MEMORIES

PRINT OUT A FEW PICTURES AND STICK
THEM HERE TO BRING BACK MEMORIES OF
THE SEXY EVENT

OUR SEXUAL BUCKET LIST

WHICH
TASK :

HER THOUGHTS BEFORE :   HIS THOUGHTS BEFORE :

_____   _____

_____   _____

_____   _____

_____   _____

COMPLETED

DATE :

HER THOUGHTS AFTER :   HIS THOUGHTS AFTER :

HER RATING (1 – 10)   HIS RATING (1 – 10)

I WOULD LIKE TO DO IT AGAIN   I WOULD LIKE TO DO IT AGAIN

OUR JOURNAL

DESCRIBE IN DETAIL EVERY PART OF THE EVENT
WHAT HAPPENED? HOW? WHERE? WHAT DID YOU LIKE?

PICTURES & MEMORIES

PRINT OUT A FEW PICTURES AND STICK
THEM HERE TO BRING BACK MEMORIES OF
THE SEXY EVENT

OUR SEXUAL BUCKET LIST

WHICH
TASK :

HER THOUGHTS BEFORE :

_____

_____

_____

_____

HIS THOUGHTS BEFORE :

_____

_____

_____

_____

COMPLETED

DATE :

HER THOUGHTS AFTER :

HIS THOUGHTS AFTER :

HER RATING (1 – 10)

☐

HIS RATING (1 – 10)

☐

I WOULD LIKE TO DO IT AGAIN

☐

I WOULD LIKE TO DO IT AGAIN

☐

OUR JOURNAL

DESCRIBE IN DETAIL EVERY PART OF THE EVENT
WHAT HAPPENED? HOW? WHERE? WHAT DID YOU LIKE?

_____

_____

_____

_____

_____

_____

_____

_____

_____

_____

_____

_____

_____

_____

_____

_____

_____

_____

_____

PICTURES & MEMORIES

PRINT OUT A FEW PICTURES AND STICK
THEM HERE TO BRING BACK MEMORIES OF
THE SEXY EVENT

OUR SEXUAL BUCKET LIST

WHICH
TASK :

HER THOUGHTS BEFORE :

HIS THOUGHTS BEFORE :

_____

_____

_____

_____

_____

_____

_____

_____

COMPLETED

DATE :

HER THOUGHTS AFTER :

HIS THOUGHTS AFTER :

HER RATING (1 – 10)

HIS RATING (1 – 10)

I WOULD LIKE TO DO IT AGAIN

I WOULD LIKE TO DO IT AGAIN

OUR JOURNAL

DESCRIBE IN DETAIL EVERY PART OF THE EVENT
WHAT HAPPENED? HOW? WHERE? WHAT DID YOU LIKE?

_____

_____

_____

_____

_____

_____

_____

_____

_____

_____

_____

_____

_____

_____

_____

_____

_____

_____

PICTURES & MEMORIES

PRINT OUT A FEW PICTURES AND STICK
THEM HERE TO BRING BACK MEMORIES OF
THE SEXY EVENT

OUR SEXUAL BUCKET LIST

WHICH
TASK :

HER THOUGHTS BEFORE :   HIS THOUGHTS BEFORE :

_____   _____

_____   _____

_____   _____

_____   _____

COMPLETED

DATE :

HER THOUGHTS AFTER :   HIS THOUGHTS AFTER :

HER RATING (1 – 10)   HIS RATING (1 – 10)

[ ]   [ ]

I WOULD LIKE TO DO IT AGAIN   I WOULD LIKE TO DO IT AGAIN

[ ]   [ ]

OUR JOURNAL

DESCRIBE IN DETAIL EVERY PART OF THE EVENT
WHAT HAPPENED? HOW? WHERE? WHAT DID YOU LIKE?

PICTURES & MEMORIES

PRINT OUT A FEW PICTURES AND STICK
THEM HERE TO BRING BACK MEMORIES OF
THE SEXY EVENT

OUR SEXUAL BUCKET LIST

WHICH
TASK :

HER THOUGHTS BEFORE :

HIS THOUGHTS BEFORE :

_____

_____

_____

_____

_____

_____

_____

_____

COMPLETED

DATE :

HER THOUGHTS AFTER :

HIS THOUGHTS AFTER :

HER RATING (1 – 10)

HIS RATING (1 – 10)

I WOULD LIKE TO DO IT AGAIN

I WOULD LIKE TO DO IT AGAIN

OUR JOURNAL

_____

_____

_____

_____

_____

_____

_____

_____

_____

_____

_____

_____

_____

_____

_____

_____

_____

PICTURES & MEMORIES

PRINT OUT A FEW PICTURES AND STICK
THEM HERE TO BRING BACK MEMORIES OF
THE SEXY EVENT

OUR SEXUAL BUCKET LIST

WHICH
TASK :

HER THOUGHTS BEFORE :

_____

_____

_____

_____

HIS THOUGHTS BEFORE :

_____

_____

_____

_____

COMPLETED

DATE :

HER THOUGHTS AFTER :

HIS THOUGHTS AFTER :

HER RATING (1 – 10)

☐

HIS RATING (1 – 10)

☐

I WOULD LIKE TO DO IT AGAIN

☐

I WOULD LIKE TO DO IT AGAIN

☐

OUR JOURNAL

DESCRIBE IN DETAIL EVERY PART OF THE EVENT
WHAT HAPPENED? HOW? WHERE? WHAT DID YOU LIKE?

PICTURES & MEMORIES

PRINT OUT A FEW PICTURES AND STICK
THEM HERE TO BRING BACK MEMORIES OF
THE SEXY EVENT

OUR SEXUAL BUCKET LIST

WHICH
TASK :

HER THOUGHTS BEFORE :

HIS THOUGHTS BEFORE :

_____

_____

_____

_____

_____

_____

_____

_____

COMPLETED

DATE :

HER THOUGHTS AFTER :

HIS THOUGHTS AFTER :

HER RATING (1 – 10)

HIS RATING (1 – 10)

I WOULD LIKE TO DO IT AGAIN

I WOULD LIKE TO DO IT AGAIN

OUR JOURNAL

DESCRIBE IN DETAIL EVERY PART OF THE EVENT
WHAT HAPPENED? HOW? WHERE? WHAT DID YOU LIKE?

_____

_____

_____

_____

_____

_____

_____

_____

_____

_____

_____

_____

_____

_____

_____

_____

_____

_____

_____

_____

_____

_____

PICTURES & MEMORIES

PRINT OUT A FEW PICTURES AND STICK
THEM HERE TO BRING BACK MEMORIES OF
THE SEXY EVENT

OUR SEXUAL BUCKET LIST

WHICH
TASK :

HER THOUGHTS BEFORE :

HIS THOUGHTS BEFORE :

_____

_____

_____

_____

_____

_____

_____

COMPLETED

DATE :

HER THOUGHTS AFTER :

HIS THOUGHTS AFTER :

HER RATING (1 – 10)

HIS RATING (1 – 10)

I WOULD LIKE TO DO IT AGAIN

I WOULD LIKE TO DO IT AGAI

OUR JOURNAL

DESCRIBE IN DETAIL EVERY PART OF THE EVENT
WHAT HAPPENED? HOW? WHERE? WHAT DID YOU LIKE?

PICTURES & MEMORIES

PRINT OUT A FEW PICTURES AND STICK
THEM HERE TO BRING BACK MEMORIES OF
THE SEXY EVENT

OUR SEXUAL BUCKET LIST

WHICH
TASK :

HER THOUGHTS BEFORE :

HIS THOUGHTS BEFORE :

_____

_____

_____

_____

_____

_____

_____

_____

COMPLETED

DATE :

HER THOUGHTS AFTER :

HIS THOUGHTS AFTER :

HER RATING (1 – 10)

HIS RATING (1 – 10)

I WOULD LIKE TO DO IT AGAIN

I WOULD LIKE TO DO IT AGAIN

OUR JOURNAL

DESCRIBE IN DETAIL EVERY PART OF THE EVENT
WHAT HAPPENED? HOW? WHERE? WHAT DID YOU LIKE?

_____

_____

_____

_____

_____

_____

_____

_____

_____

_____

_____

_____

_____

_____

_____

_____

_____

_____

PICTURES & MEMORIES

PRINT OUT A FEW PICTURES AND STICK
THEM HERE TO BRING BACK MEMORIES OF
THE SEXY EVENT

OUR SEXUAL BUCKET LIST

WHICH
TASK :

HER THOUGHTS BEFORE :

HIS THOUGHTS BEFORE :

_____

_____

_____

_____

_____

_____

_____

COMPLETED

DATE :

HER THOUGHTS AFTER :

HIS THOUGHTS AFTER :

HER RATING (1 – 10)

HIS RATING (1 – 10)

☐

☐

I WOULD LIKE TO DO IT AGAIN

I WOULD LIKE TO DO IT AGAIN

☐

☐

OUR JOURNAL

DESCRIBE IN DETAIL EVERY PART OF THE EVENT
WHAT HAPPENED? HOW? WHERE? WHAT DID YOU LIKE?

PICTURES & MEMORIES

PRINT OUT A FEW PICTURES AND STICK
THEM HERE TO BRING BACK MEMORIES OF
THE SEXY EVENT

OUR SEXUAL BUCKET LIST

WHICH
TASK :

HER THOUGHTS BEFORE :

HIS THOUGHTS BEFORE :

_____

_____

_____

_____

_____

_____

_____

_____

COMPLETED

DATE :

HER THOUGHTS AFTER :

HIS THOUGHTS AFTER :

HER RATING (1 – 10)

HIS RATING (1 – 10)

I WOULD LIKE TO DO IT AGAIN

I WOULD LIKE TO DO IT AGAIN

OUR JOURNAL

DESCRIBE IN DETAIL EVERY PART OF THE EVENT
WHAT HAPPENED? HOW? WHERE? WHAT DID YOU LIKE?

_____

_____

_____

_____

_____

_____

_____

_____

_____

_____

_____

_____

_____

_____

_____

_____

_____

_____

_____

PICTURES & MEMORIES

PRINT OUT A FEW PICTURES AND STICK
THEM HERE TO BRING BACK MEMORIES OF
THE SEXY EVENT

OUR SEXUAL BUCKET LIST

WHICH
TASK :

HER THOUGHTS BEFORE :

_____

_____

_____

_____

HIS THOUGHTS BEFORE :

_____

_____

_____

_____

COMPLETED

DATE :

HER THOUGHTS AFTER :

HIS THOUGHTS AFTER :

HER RATING (1 – 10)

☐

HIS RATING (1 – 10)

☐

I WOULD LIKE TO DO IT AGAIN

☐

I WOULD LIKE TO DO IT AGAIN

☐

OUR JOURNAL

PICTURES & MEMORIES

PRINT OUT A FEW PICTURES AND STICK
THEM HERE TO BRING BACK MEMORIES OF
THE SEXY EVENT

OUR SEXUAL BUCKET LIST

WHICH
TASK :

HER THOUGHTS BEFORE :   HIS THOUGHTS BEFORE :

COMPLETED

DATE :

HER THOUGHTS AFTER :   HIS THOUGHTS AFTER :

HER RATING (1 – 10)   HIS RATING (1 – 10)

I WOULD LIKE TO DO IT AGAIN   I WOULD LIKE TO DO IT AGAIN

OUR JOURNAL

DESCRIBE IN DETAIL EVERY PART OF THE EVENT
WHAT HAPPENED? HOW? WHERE? WHAT DID YOU LIKE?

_____

_____

_____

_____

_____

_____

_____

_____

_____

_____

_____

_____

_____

_____

_____

_____

_____

_____

PICTURES & MEMORIES

PRINT OUT A FEW PICTURES AND STICK
THEM HERE TO BRING BACK MEMORIES OF
THE SEXY EVENT

OUR SEXUAL BUCKET LIST

WHICH
TASK :

HER THOUGHTS BEFORE :

HIS THOUGHTS BEFORE :

_____

_____

_____

_____

_____

_____

_____

COMPLETED

DATE :

HER THOUGHTS AFTER :

HIS THOUGHTS AFTER :

HER RATING (1 – 10)

HIS RATING (1 – 10)

I WOULD LIKE TO DO IT AGAIN

I WOULD LIKE TO DO IT AGAI

OUR JOURNAL

DESCRIBE IN DETAIL EVERY PART OF THE EVENT
WHAT HAPPENED? HOW? WHERE? WHAT DID YOU LIKE?

_____

_____

_____

_____

_____

_____

_____

_____

_____

_____

_____

_____

_____

_____

_____

_____

_____

_____

_____

_____

PICTURES & MEMORIES

PRINT OUT A FEW PICTURES AND STICK
THEM HERE TO BRING BACK MEMORIES OF
THE SEXY EVENT

OUR SEXUAL BUCKET LIST

WHICH
TASK :

HER THOUGHTS BEFORE :

HIS THOUGHTS BEFORE :

_____

_____

_____

_____

_____

_____

_____

_____

COMPLETED

DATE :

HER THOUGHTS AFTER :

HIS THOUGHTS AFTER :

HER RATING (1 – 10)

HIS RATING (1 – 10)

I WOULD LIKE TO DO IT AGAIN

I WOULD LIKE TO DO IT AGAIN

OUR JOURNAL

DESCRIBE IN DETAIL EVERY PART OF THE EVENT
WHAT HAPPENED? HOW? WHERE? WHAT DID YOU LIKE?

PICTURES & MEMORIES

PRINT OUT A FEW PICTURES AND STICK
THEM HERE TO BRING BACK MEMORIES OF
THE SEXY EVENT

OUR SEXUAL BUCKET LIST

WHICH
TASK :

HER THOUGHTS BEFORE :   HIS THOUGHTS BEFORE :

_____   _____

_____   _____

_____   _____

_____   _____

COMPLETED

DATE :

HER THOUGHTS AFTER :   HIS THOUGHTS AFTER :

HER RATING (1 – 10)   HIS RATING (1 – 10)

☐   ☐

I WOULD LIKE TO DO IT AGAIN   I WOULD LIKE TO DO IT AGAIN

☐   ☐

OUR JOURNAL

PICTURES & MEMORIES

PRINT OUT A FEW PICTURES AND STICK
THEM HERE TO BRING BACK MEMORIES OF
THE SEXY EVENT

OUR SEXUAL BUCKET LIST

WHICH
TASK :

HER THOUGHTS BEFORE :

HIS THOUGHTS BEFORE :

_____

_____

_____

_____

_____

_____

_____

_____

COMPLETED

DATE :

HER THOUGHTS AFTER :

HIS THOUGHTS AFTER :

HER RATING (1 – 10)

HIS RATING (1 – 10)

I WOULD LIKE TO DO IT AGAIN

I WOULD LIKE TO DO IT AGAIN

OUR JOURNAL

_____

_____

_____

_____

_____

_____

_____

_____

_____

_____

_____

_____

_____

_____

_____

_____

_____

_____

_____

_____

_____

PICTURES & MEMORIES

PRINT OUT A FEW PICTURES AND STICK
THEM HERE TO BRING BACK MEMORIES OF
THE SEXY EVENT

OUR SEXUAL BUCKET LIST

WHICH
TASK :

HER THOUGHTS BEFORE :

HIS THOUGHTS BEFORE :

_____

_____

_____

_____

_____

_____

_____

_____

COMPLETED

DATE :

HER THOUGHTS AFTER :

HIS THOUGHTS AFTER :

HER RATING (1 – 10)

HIS RATING (1 – 10)

I WOULD LIKE TO DO IT AGAIN

I WOULD LIKE TO DO IT AGAIN

OUR JOURNAL

DESCRIBE IN DETAIL EVERY PART OF THE EVENT
WHAT HAPPENED? HOW? WHERE? WHAT DID YOU LIKE?

PICTURES & MEMORIES

PRINT OUT A FEW PICTURES AND STICK
THEM HERE TO BRING BACK MEMORIES OF
THE SEXY EVENT

OUR SEXUAL BUCKET LIST

WHICH
TASK :

HER THOUGHTS BEFORE :

HIS THOUGHTS BEFORE :

_____

_____

_____

_____

_____

_____

_____

_____

COMPLETED

DATE :

HER THOUGHTS AFTER :

HIS THOUGHTS AFTER :

HER RATING (1 – 10)

HIS RATING (1 – 10)

I WOULD LIKE TO DO IT AGAIN

I WOULD LIKE TO DO IT AGAIN

OUR JOURNAL

DESCRIBE IN DETAIL EVERY PART OF THE EVENT
WHAT HAPPENED? HOW? WHERE? WHAT DID YOU LIKE?

_____

_____

_____

_____

_____

_____

_____

_____

_____

_____

_____

_____

_____

_____

_____

_____

_____

_____

PICTURES & MEMORIES

PRINT OUT A FEW PICTURES AND STICK
THEM HERE TO BRING BACK MEMORIES OF
THE SEXY EVENT

OUR SEXUAL BUCKET LIST

WHICH
TASK :

HER THOUGHTS BEFORE :

HIS THOUGHTS BEFORE :

_____

_____

_____

_____

_____

_____

_____

_____

COMPLETED

DATE :

HER THOUGHTS AFTER :

HIS THOUGHTS AFTER :

HER RATING (1 – 10)

HIS RATING (1 – 10)

I WOULD LIKE TO DO IT AGAIN

I WOULD LIKE TO DO IT AGAIN

OUR JOURNAL

DESCRIBE IN DETAIL EVERY PART OF THE EVENT
WHAT HAPPENED? HOW? WHERE? WHAT DID YOU LIKE?

PICTURES & MEMORIES

PRINT OUT A FEW PICTURES AND STICK
THEM HERE TO BRING BACK MEMORIES OF
THE SEXY EVENT

OUR SEXUAL BUCKET LIST

WHICH
TASK :

HER THOUGHTS BEFORE :

HIS THOUGHTS BEFORE :

_____

_____

_____

_____

_____

_____

_____

_____

COMPLETED

DATE :

HER THOUGHTS AFTER :

HIS THOUGHTS AFTER :

HER RATING (1 – 10)

HIS RATING (1 – 10)

I WOULD LIKE TO DO IT AGAIN

I WOULD LIKE TO DO IT AGAIN

OUR JOURNAL

_____

_____

_____

_____

_____

_____

_____

_____

_____

_____

_____

_____

_____

_____

_____

_____

_____

_____

PICTURES & MEMORIES

PRINT OUT A FEW PICTURES AND STICK
THEM HERE TO BRING BACK MEMORIES OF
THE SEXY EVENT

OUR SEXUAL BUCKET LIST

WHICH
TASK :

HER THOUGHTS BEFORE :

HIS THOUGHTS BEFORE :

_____

_____

_____

_____

_____

_____

_____

_____

COMPLETED

DATE :

HER THOUGHTS AFTER :

HIS THOUGHTS AFTER :

HER RATING (1 – 10)

HIS RATING (1 – 10)

I WOULD LIKE TO DO IT AGAIN

I WOULD LIKE TO DO IT AGAIN

OUR JOURNAL

DESCRIBE IN DETAIL EVERY PART OF THE EVENT
WHAT HAPPENED? HOW? WHERE? WHAT DID YOU LIKE?

PICTURES & MEMORIES

PRINT OUT A FEW PICTURES AND STICK
THEM HERE TO BRING BACK MEMORIES OF
THE SEXY EVENT

OUR SEXUAL BUCKET LIST

WHICH
  TASK :

HER THOUGHTS BEFORE :   HIS THOUGHTS BEFORE :

_____   _____

_____   _____

_____   _____

_____   _____

COMPLETED

DATE :

HER THOUGHTS AFTER :   HIS THOUGHTS AFTER :

HER RATING (1 – 10)   HIS RATING (1 – 10)

☐   ☐

I WOULD LIKE TO DO IT AGAIN   I WOULD LIKE TO DO IT AGAIN

☐   ☐

OUR JOURNAL

DESCRIBE IN DETAIL EVERY PART OF THE EVENT
WHAT HAPPENED? HOW? WHERE? WHAT DID YOU LIKE?

_____

_____

_____

_____

_____

_____

_____

_____

_____

_____

_____

_____

_____

_____

_____

_____

_____

_____

_____

_____

_____

PICTURES & MEMORIES

PRINT OUT A FEW PICTURES AND STICK
THEM HERE TO BRING BACK MEMORIES OF
THE SEXY EVENT

OUR SEXUAL BUCKET LIST

WHICH
TASK :

HER THOUGHTS BEFORE :

HIS THOUGHTS BEFORE :

_____

_____

_____

_____

_____

_____

_____

COMPLETED

DATE :

HER THOUGHTS AFTER :

HIS THOUGHTS AFTER :

HER RATING (1 – 10)

HIS RATING (1 – 10)

I WOULD LIKE TO DO IT AGAIN

I WOULD LIKE TO DO IT AGAIN

OUR JOURNAL

DESCRIBE IN DETAIL EVERY PART OF THE EVENT
WHAT HAPPENED? HOW? WHERE? WHAT DID YOU LIKE?

PICTURES & MEMORIES

PRINT OUT A FEW PICTURES AND STICK
THEM HERE TO BRING BACK MEMORIES OF
THE SEXY EVENT

OUR SEXUAL BUCKET LIST

WHICH
TASK :

HER THOUGHTS BEFORE :

_____

_____

_____

_____

HIS THOUGHTS BEFORE :

_____

_____

_____

_____

COMPLETED

DATE :

HER THOUGHTS AFTER :

HIS THOUGHTS AFTER :

HER RATING (1 – 10)

☐

HIS RATING (1 – 10)

☐

I WOULD LIKE TO DO IT AGAIN

☐

I WOULD LIKE TO DO IT AGAIN

☐

OUR JOURNAL

_____

_____

_____

_____

_____

_____

_____

_____

_____

_____

_____

_____

_____

_____

_____

_____

_____

_____

PICTURES & MEMORIES

PRINT OUT A FEW PICTURES AND STICK
THEM HERE TO BRING BACK MEMORIES OF
THE SEXY EVENT

Made in the USA
Monee, IL
25 February 2023

28671400R10066